Charles Edmonds

# Venus and Adonis, from the Hitherto Unknown ed. of 1599

The passionate pilgrime, from the first ed. of 1599; of which only two

copies are known; Epigrammes

*THE ISHAM REPRINTS.*

# THE PASSIONATE PILGRIME.

## 1599.

# THE PASSIONATE PILGRIME,

A COLLECTION OF FUGITIVE POETRY PUBLISHED

UNDER THE NAME OF SHAKESPEARE.

*NEW EDITION*,

ACCURATELY REPRINTED FROM THE ORIGINAL

IMPRESSION OF 1599, IN THE

POSSESSION OF

SIR CHARLES ISHAM, Bart.

WITH A PREFACE,

IN WHICH THE CLAIMS OF RICHARD BARNFIELD TO THE

AUTHORSHIP OF TWO OF THE PIECES ARE

VINDICATED FROM THE OBJECTIONS

OF MR. J. PAYNE COLLIER,

BY CHARLES EDMONDS,

EDITOR OF THE POETRY OF THE

ANTI-JACOBIN.

LONDON:

PRINTED AT THE CHISWICK PRESS.

1870.

# EDITOR'S PREFACE.

THIS remarkable collection of fugitive pieces, publifhed under a fanciful title to diftinguifh it from fimilar mifcellanies, as well as probably to induce the public to fuppofe that the whole was a new poem by Shakefpeare, although purporting to be folely his production, really confifts of poems by various contemporary writers. In the words of Mr. Dyce, in the Memoir prefixed to Shakefpeare's Sonnets, lxxvii. ed. Pickering, 1832: "'The Paffionate Pilgrime' appears to have been given to the prefs without his confent or even his knowledge, and how much of it proceeded from his pen cannot be diftinctly afcertained." But the object of the publifher, William Jaggard, in thus attributing the whole to Shakefpeare is fufficiently apparent;—the poet's great popularity would be likely to make the publication a fuccefsful venture, while his known indifference to the fate of his works would render his calling attention to the fraud extremely improbable.

That William Jaggard was generally unfcrupulous in his bufinefs tranfactions is fhown by his conduct in the publication of another edition of this work, called on the title-page " the third," printed in 1612. The

" fecond" edition feems to have difappeared altogether, no copy being known to exift. This third impreffion contains all the poems that appeared in that of 1599, and here again all are attributed to Shakefpeare, notwithftanding it muft have been known by this time that the whole could not have been his production. But Jaggard, not content with his firft deception on the public, has here, with an effrontery almoft ludicrous, ventured to add to the original title the expreffion,— " or, Certaine Amorous Sonnets between Venus and Adonis;" although only four of them bear upon thofe perfonages; his intention evidently being to take advantage of the celebrity of the poem bearing their names. He, however, foon met with his match, in confequence of having without authority inferted in the fame volume two of Ovid's Epiftles, which, from the ambiguous wording of the title-page, might alfo be fuppofed to have been from the pen of Shakefpeare. Thefe had really been tranflated by Thomas Heywood, as was no doubt known to Jaggard, he having been the printer of the work in which they appeared, and which was publifhed with Heywood's name in 1609, under the title of " Troia Britannica, or Great Britaines Troy; a Poem, etc. London, printed by W. Jaggard:" folio. What fteps Heywood, who was more fenfitive than Shakefpeare on the fcore of his publications, took in the matter, will appear further on.

I am the more particular in thus calling attention to the natural laxity of Jaggard's principles, as it will enable us to judge how he would act in any other inftance in which his intereft was concerned: as to the prefent publication, unfortunately, his equivocal proceedings have been the means of involving an interefting literary ſubject in conſiderable doubt, and of throwing obloquy on parties little deſerving of it.

That we may underſtand the peculiar bearings of the caſe, I will give a complete liſt of the various pieces of which "The Paſſionate Pilgrime" conſiſts, with references to the work in which each firſt appeared, followed by a few obſervations on Barnfield's ſhare in it.

### [I.]

" *When my Loue ſweares that ſhe is made of truth.*" This, with ſome verbal variations, is the ſame as No. 138 of Shakeſpeare's Sonnets.

### [II.]

" *Two Loues I haue, of Comfort, and Deſpaire.*" This poem, alſo, with ſome ſlight variations, is the ſame as Sonnet 144.

### [III.]

" *Did not the heauenly Rhetorike of thine eie.*" With ſome trifling variations this occurs in " Love's Labour's Loſt," 1598.

### [IV.]

" *Sweet Cytherea, ſitting by a Brooke.*" Is found only in " The Paſſionate Pilgrime."

### [V.]

" *If Loue make me forſworn, how ſhal I ſwere to loue.*" Printed, with ſlight variations, in " Love's Labour's Loſt," 1598.

### [VI.]

" *Scarſe had the Sunne dride up the deawy morne.*" Occurs only in " The Paſſionate Pilgrime."

### [VII.]

" *Faire is my loue, but not ſo faire as fickle.*" Found only in " The Paſſionate Pilgrime."

[VIII.]

" *If Muficke and fweet Poetrie agree.*" This Sonnet
is taken from a fmall collection of poems by Richard
Barnfield, entitled " The Encomion of Lady Pecunia,"
printed in 1598. It occurs in the latter portion,
called " Poems : in diuers humors," with the following
heading: " To his friend Maifter R. L. In praife of
Mufique and Poetrie," but is omitted in the fecond
edition in 1605, entitled " Lady Pecunia."

[IX.]

" *Faire was the morne, when the faire Queene of
loue.*" Occurs only in " The Paffionate Pilgrime."

[X.]

" *Sweet Rofe, faire flower, vntimely pluckt, foon
vaded.*" This likewife occurs only in " The Paffionate
Pilgrime."

[IX.]

" *Venus, with Adonis fitting by her.*" This fonnet,
with fome variations, including the following lines (9
to 14) which are fubftituted for thofe in " The Paffionate Pilgrime," occurs in B. Griffin's rare collection
of feventy-two fonnets, printed under the title of
" Fideffa," in 1596 :—

> " But he a wayward boy refufde her offer,
>    And ran away, the beautious Queene neglecting :
> Shewing both folly to abufe her proffer,
>    And all his fex of cowardife detecting.
> Oh that I had my miftris at that bay,
> To kiffe and clippe me till I ranne away ! "

But the Rev. R. Greene, of Lichfield, in a commu-
nication to " Notes and Queries," vol. x. 1ft fer. con-
tends, with much plaufibility, that the authorfhip fhould
be given to Shakefpeare.

[xii.]

" *Crabbed age and youth cannot live together.*" Although the verſion in " The Paſſionate Pilgrime " is the firſt with which we are acquainted, yet it is probable that it made its appearance earlier, in Deloney's "Garland of Good Will," which was printed in or about 1596; but as no edition of ſo early a date is extant, it is impoſſible to ſpeak with certainty. At any rate, it is included, with variations, in ſeveral ſubſequent impreſſions of that popular work.

[xiii.]

" *Beauty is but a vaine and doubtfull good.*" Occurs only in " The Paſſionate Pilgrime."

[xiv.]

" *Good night, good reſt, ah neither be my ſhare.*" Occurs only in " The Paſſionate Pilgrime."

[xv.]

" *Lord howe mine eies throw gazes to the eaſt.*" Occurs only in " The Paſſionate Pilgrime."

[xvi.]

" *It was a lording's daughter, the faireſt one of three.*" Occurs only in "The Paſſionate Pilgrime."

[xvii.]

" *On a day alack the day.*" This poem is printed in "Love's Labour's Loſt," 1598. It occurs alſo in "England's Helicon," (a miſcellany of poetry, firſt publiſhed in 1600,) with Shakeſpeare's name appended to it. Both in the latter and in " The Paſſionate Pilgrime," the following two lines, forming the laſt couplet but one, are omitted :—

> "Thou for whom Jove would ſwear
> Juno but an Ethiop were."

[xviii.]

" *My flocks feed not.*" This poem had, two years
before, in 1597, with flight variations, appeared anony-
moufly, with the mufic, in a collection of Madrigals,
by Thomas Weelkes. It is printed alfo, with corrections,—
fuch as *moan* for *woe* in the laft line but three,—in
" England's Helicon," 1600, being there entitled " The
unknowne Sheepheard's Complaint," and fubfcribed
*Ignoto*, a proof that Bodenham, the editor, was then
unacquainted with the name of the author, but difin-
clined to attribute it to Shakefpeare, as had been done
in " The Paffionate Pilgrime," the year before, or to
Weelkes, in whofe collection it firft appeared.

[xix.]

" *When as thine eie hath chofe the dame.*" Occurs
only in " The Paffionate Pilgrime." But Mr. Halliwell,
in his folio Shakefpeare, vol. 16, p. 466-7, fays, " A
very early manufcript copy of this poem, with many
variations, is preferved in a poetical mifcellany, com-
piled, I believe, fome years before the appearance of
' The Paffionate Pilgrime.' "

[xx.]

" *Live with me and be my love.*" This poem is
affigned by name to Chriftopher Marlowe in " Eng-
land's Helicon," 1600, and what is called " Love's
Anfwere" appears in the fame collection, under the
name of *Ignoto*, a fignature fometimes adopted by Sir
Walter Raleigh. They are, befides, attributed to thefe
authors in Walton's " Angler," under the titles of
" The Milk-maid's Song," and " The Milk-maid's
Mother's Anfwer." Both, however, as printed in
" The Paffionate Pilgrime," and in " England's Heli-
con," are incomplete, but they are printed at length in
Percy's " Reliques."

[xxi.]

" *As it fell upon a day.*" This ode, like No. 8, is printed as Barnfield's, among his "Poems: in diuers humors," 1598. It alfo appears in "England's Helicon," 1600, following " My flocks feed not," and is entitled " Another of the fame Sheepheardes." From this latter obfervation, and his figning both *Ignoto*, the editor, Bodenham, not only avows his inability to point out the real authors, but difallows the claims equally of Barnfield, Shakefpeare, and Weelkes, under whofe refpective names they had been publifhed fo fhort a time before; another proof of the laxity of editing and publifhing in thofe days.

[xxi*.]

" *Whilft as fickle fortune fmiled.*" Mr. Collier, in his firft edition of Shakefpeare, 1843, vol. 8, note, pp. 577-8, thus remarks on this poem: " It is a feparate production, both in fubject and place, with a divifion between it and Barnfield's poem which precedes it; neverthelefs they have been incautioufly coupled in fome modern editions." In his fecond edition, 1858, vol. 6, p. 692, note, publifhed after he had changed his previous opinion that Barnfield was the rightful owner, he thus varies his dictum: " It is a feparate production, both in fubject and place, with a flight divifion (but no heading) between it and the poem which precedes it: neverthelefs they have been coupled in fome modern editions, moft likely becaufe they are found erroneoufly united in Barnfield's ' Encomion,' 1598."

So far from thefe being two feparate productions, my impreffion is that they were originally intended for one, and cannot otherwife be confidered without a direct violation of propriety. If we refer to Barnfield's "Encomion" of 1598, we find that the lines beginning "As it fell vpon a Day," down to "Faithfull friend, from flatt'ring foe," form one continuous poem, without any break or any interruption of the fenfe, extending over three pages, and bearing the general title "An Ode." Had they been intended for two poems, they could eafily have been arranged fo; there is not only plenty of room for the purpofe, but the book throughout is printed with fuch accuracy as to induce a fuppofition that it was produced under the author's own infpection. On the other hand, no certain inference that they fhould form two poems inftead of one can be drawn from the manner in which they appear in "The Paffionate Pilgrime;" for in this work, as we fee, there is no heading to any of the pieces, and the printer has ufed his own difcretion in the arrangement of each page; confequently it is only by the context that we can determine where one piece ends and another begins. Applying this teft to the prefent cafe, I think we cannot avoid the conclufion that the author wrote thefe lines as one ode, and that by dividing it into two, as Mr. Collier does, we deftroy the whole fequence and moral, making the firft portion end with as much unintelligible abruptnefs as the fecond begins. The poet's object being to fhow the fimilarity of his griefs to thofe of the nightingale, he devotes the lines terminating with the word "forrowing" to the bird; he then takes up his own woes with the line beginning "Whilft as fickle fortune fmiled," and enlarges upon them to the end of the ode. This view is confirmed by the fucceeding line, "Thou and I were both beguiled," which, on any other hypothefis would be, as I have already faid, un-intelligible.   It is moreover more logical to put faith in what has evidently been prepared with care than in a reprint which is confeffedly an unauthorized and fraudu-lent impreffion.   It fhould be noticed that Mr. Halli-well, in his folio Shakefpeare, prints them as two poems, but Mr. Knight as one.

Another curious circumftance occurs with regard to this ode.   The reprint of it in " England's Helicon," 1600, interpolates, after the line " Carelefs of thy for-rowing," the following couplet :

> " Even fo, poore bird like thee,
> None a-live will pitty mee."

And thus the poem, in that publication, terminates, although the lines are fo appropriate to the fubjeft, and fo well adapted to fupply a miffing link of conneftion between the firft and fecond portions of the ode, that we might almoft affume they had been introduced for this purpofe.   But as this is not the cafe, we are driven to the conclufion that the editor of " England's Heli-con," inftead of following Barnfield's publication, where he would have found the ode complete, made ufe of that in " The Paffionate Pilgrime," imagining that it terminated, as there printed, at the bottom of the page. But feeling, like moft readers, probably, that this ending was too abrupt for the fubjeft, and falling into the fame error as Mr. Collier, that the lines on the next page began a new ode, he added the couplet in queftion as a more appropriate termination, experiencing as little compunftion in the matter as Bifhop Percy did in " im-proving " the old ballads in his " Reliques."   Although Mr. Dyce, Mr. Collier, Mr. C. Knight, and other able editors, point out this interpolation, they do not feem to think it worthy the attention which I believe it deferves. This couplet does not appear in "The Paffionate Pilgrime" of 1612.

It appears, therefore, from the above enumeration, that only five out of the twenty-one pieces forming "The Paffionate Pilgrime" poffefs anything like direct evidence of being from Shakefpeare's hand, and this confifts in their firft appearance in his acknowledged works, in their general refemblance to his other compofitions, and in the abfence of other claimants. Though eleven of the others are printed in "The Paffionate Pilgrime," for, as far as we yet know, the firft time, there is no ground whatever beyond the affertion on its title-page for attributing them to Shakefpeare, while the flender merit of feveral of them decidedly negatives this affumption ; the authorfhip of thefe, confequently, is ftill uncertain ; while as to the remaining five, if any weight is to be allowed to fuch ftrong claims as thofe founded on priority of publication by competent living authors, three muft be affigned, as heretofore, to Barnfield and Griffin ; one is no doubt, as is generally affumed, the work of Marlowe, and the laft, which is quite unworthy of Shakefpeare, was probably an anonymous piece, merely fet to mufic by Weelkes.

Whatever may be thought of the claims of the other poets to their refpective pieces, thofe of Barnfield to the authorfhip of "If Mufique and fweet Poetrie agree," and "As it fell upon a day," have been recently ftrongly contefted by Mr. Collier, and the honour affigned to Shakefpeare, notwithftanding that in his firft edition of our great bard, he believes in Barnfield's own affertion of parentage, and difagrees with Bofwell, who had fuggefted that John Jaggard, in 1598, might have ftolen Shakefpeare's verfes, and attributed them to Barnfield. His reafons for this change of opinion feem to me fo infufficient, and fo derogatory to the honefty as well as to the common fenfe of Barnfield, that I think it only fair to the latter to give them a little confideration ; while, on the other hand, to do no injuftice to Mr. Collier, I will firft quote his own lateft words on the fubject, as they ftand in his valuable " Bibliographical and Critical Account of the Rareft Books in the Englifh Language," 2 vols. 8vo. 1865 :

" It is no fmall tribute to Barnfield that two poems printed by him, or for him, in 1598, having in the next year been inferted in Shakefpeare's ' Paffionate Pil- grim,' were long thought by many to be the property of Barnfield, on account of his priority of claim. In 1598 the fine fonnet in praife of Dowland and Spenfer, ' If mufic and fweet poetry agree,' and the beautiful lyric, ' As it fell upon a day,' were firft publifhed as Barn- field's, in a work which then bore the following title :

" ' The Encomion of Lady Pecunia, or The praife of Money.—*quærenda pecunia primum eft, virtus poft nummos.*—London, Printed by G. S. for Iohn Iaggard, and are to be folde at his fhoppe neere Temple-barre, at the Signe of the Hand & ftarre. 1598.' (4to.)

" John Jaggard, who publifhed the above, was brother [or fon] to W. Jaggard, who publifhed Shakefpeare's ' Paffionate Pilgrim,' and in fome unexplained manner the two poems we have defignated, ' If mufic and fweet poetry agree,' and ' As it fell upon a day,' the authorfhip of our great dramatift, found their way out of the hands of W. Jaggard into thofe of John Jaggard, who, we may fuppofe, was in 1598 on the point of publifhing Barnfield's ' Encomion of Lady Pecunia : ' there he inferted them ; but they, nevertheleſs, made their appearance in 1599 in ' The Paſſionate Pilgrim,' by which it was made to feem as if W. Jaggard had ſtolen the poems from J. Jaggard, becauſe the latter had printed them as Barnfield's in the year preceding. The reverſe was, however, the faĉt ; and the matter ſtood thus doubt- fully until the year 1605, when Barnfield (perhaps partly on this account) putting forth a new impreſſion of his ' Encomion ' under a different title, and with many important changes, expreſsly excluded from that re-impreſſion the two poems, which he knew did not belong to him, and which he preſumed were the pro- perty of Shakeſpeare.

" Hence the eſpecial value of the ſecond edition of the ' Encomion,' ſince it may be ſaid to aſcertain that John Jaggard, wiſhing to ſwell Barnfield's ſmall volume in 1598, did ſo by inſerting in it two pieces that did not belong to the author of the reſt. The ſecond edi- tion of Barnfield's ' Encomion,' under the title of ' Lady Pecunia, or the praiſe of Money,' was not known at all until a comparatively recent date ; and ſtill more re- cently it was diſcovered that it did not contain the poems to which Barnfield ſeemed to have the earlieſt title. In 1605 Barnfield was too honeſt to retain what had been improperly attributed to him in 1598. The Sonnet and the Poem are therefore not to be traced in the volume in our hands, which forms part of the library of Bridgewater Houſe."

Surely no poet was ever deprived of his rightful pro- perty on lighter grounds than are here adduced by Mr. Collier for this ſummary ſpoliation of Barnfield. It is not that he conſiders Barnfield unequal to the compofition of the two pieces in queſtion, for in a ſubſequent paragraph he deſignates the " Encomion of Lady Pecunia" as " a very clever poem," and admits that " it is not ſurpriſing that it was popular;" but, ſolely becauſe he finds that a hitherto unknown edition of Barnfield's Poems, printed ſeven years after the firſt, omits two pieces which are contained in the firſt impreſſion, he comes to the haſty concluſion that theſe were not written by Barnfield, but relinquiſhed in a fit of repentance as quietly as, in the firſt inſtance, he had wrongfully appropriated them. As to the aſſertion that John Jaggard ſtole from his relative in order to ſwell Barnfield's volume which he was about to publiſh, this is mere conjecture: on the contrary, an inſpection of the two original volumes would ſhow the greater probability of William Jaggard having been the ſpoiler, for the purpoſe of ſwelling the proportions of " The Paſſionate Pilgrime," which is ſo ſmall in bulk that to eke it out a great part is printed only on one ſide of the leaf.

If Barnfield be really the appropriator of another man's works, the way in which he introduces his ſtolen goods is certainly remarkable, for on the back of the title-page appears the following dedication :—

" *To the learned, and accompliſht Gentleman, Maiſter Nicholas Blackleech, of Grayes Innc.*

" To you, that know the tuch of true Conceat ;
(Whoſe many gifts I neede not to repeat)
I write theſe Lines: fruits of vnriper yeares ;
Wherein my Muſe no harder Cenſure feares:
Hoping in gentle Worth, you will them take ;
Not for the gift, but for the giuers ſake."

Here in the moſt unequivocal terms Barnfield claims the whole of the poems as his own ; but with becoming

b

modefty he excufes them as being the fruits of his early years, for he was even at this time only twenty-four years old.   And as a further confirmation of the truth of his affertion, one of the difputed pieces, which is the very firft in the book, is openly addreffed to a friend, R. L., prefumed to be Richard Linch, author of " Diella," 1596, and fome Sonnets inferted in Drayton's " Legend of Robert Duke of Normandy," and in the fame poet's " Matilda."

His work begins with " Sonnet I.   To his friend Maifter R. L.   In praife of Mufique and Poetrie." Then follows, on the fame page " Sonnet II.   Againft the Difprayfers of Poetrie."   On the reverfe is " A Remembrance of fome Englifh Poets," highly laudatory of Spenfer, Daniel, Drayton, and laftly of Shakefpeare.   Immediately following this is the other difputed piece, entitled " An Ode : As it fell upon a Day," confifting of twenty-eight couplets : then lines " Written, at the requeft of a Gentleman, vnder a Gentlewoman's Picture ;" " An Epitaph vpon the Death of Sir Philip Sidney, Knight : Lord-gouernour of Vliffing ;" " An Epitaph vpon the Death of his Aunt, Miftreffe Elizabeth Skrymfher ;" concluding with, upon the top of the reverfe of the fourth leaf, " A Comparifon of the Life of Man."   The above are fo varied in ftyle as to bear out the intention of the collection, which was to confift of " Poems in divers Humours."

Although in that age literary plagiarifm was freely practifed, it is hardly likely that an author of repute like Barnfield would be fo bold as to appropriate the whole of two compofitions of peculiar merit written by another ; or aggravate a fraud liable to inftant detection by fuch an unequivocal claim to their authorfhip as he puts forth in his addrefs to Blackleech ; and the improbability is ftill greater when we confider that the perfon whom he is accufed of robbing was not only the moft noted writer of the time, but then actually living, and the object, in the very next page, of his fervent eulogy. And that this good feeling was not interrupted is evidenced by his reprinting the fame eulogy in his fecond impreffion, which would hardly have been the cafe had he, years before, been guilty towards Shakefpeare of fo unblufhing a wrong. Moreover, his difinclination to have the labours of others affigned to him is fhown by his dif-avowal in his earlier production, " Cynthia," printed in 1595, of two books imputed to him (probably Greene's " Funerals," 1594, and " Orpheus his Journey to Hell," 1595), to which his initials R. B. feem to have been fraudulently affixed. Nor is it the cafe of an unknown or incapable poet robbing his neighbour of that which he was himfelf unable to produce, for fuffi-cient poetic talent had already been fhown in his " Affectionate Shepheard," publifhed in 1594, when only twenty-one years old, and his fubfequent poems fully fuftain this early promife. He has therefore the moft effential points in his favour, namely, capability of production, diftinct affertion of authorfhip, and priority of publication ; to fay nothing of the abfence of any hoftile allufions by his contemporaries.

In his volume entitled " Cynthia" is an ode fo much refembling " As it fell upon a day," that it is almoft impoffible to doubt that both proceeded from the fame pen. It begins thus :

> " Nights were fhort, & daies were long ;
> Bloffoms on the Hauthorn's hung :
> *Philomœle* (Night-Mufiques King)
> Tolde the comming of the fpring."

Mr. Collier, in a previous article on this fubject, in-ferted in " Notes and Queries," 1856, thus fpeaks of the fecond edition of Barnfield's Poems:

" My miftaken notion, twelve years ago [he alludes to the firft edition of his Shakefpeare] was, that Barn-field, in 1605, had republifhed the whole of what had firft appeared in 1598. This is not fo. In 1605 he prefixed a general title-page, mentioning only three of the four divifions of his original work, viz. :—1. ' Lady Pecunia, or The Praife of Money.' 2. ' A Combat be-twixt Confcience and Covetoufneffe;' and 3. ' The Complaint of Poetry, or [for] the Death of Liberality.' He fays not one word about what had been his fourth divifion in 1508 [1598], ' Poems in divers humors;' but ftill, on the very laft leaf of the impreffion of 1605, Barnfield places ' A Remembrance of fome Englifh Poets,' which had appeared as one of the ' Poems in divers humors,' in 1598.   ' A Comparifon of the Life of Man,' a feven-line ftanza, is alfo reprinted; all the reft he feems purpofely to have excluded as if they were not his."

From the above ftatement it might be furmifed that Barnfield had intended to exclude from his new edition the whole of the " Poems in divers humours;" but even were this the cafe, it would not have been occa-fioned, I contend, by confcientious fcruples, but by private reafons, which fometimes influence authors even in the prefent day.   A notable inftance of fuch omiffions and alterations is to be found in Drayton's work, entitled " Idea," firft printed in 1593.   " This edition," (it is Mr. Collier, in his ' Bibliographical Account' before alluded to, who fpeaks) " deferves efpecial remark, becaufe the work fubfequently un-

derwent numerous and important changes, and more
especially becaufe it contains several poems that were
never reprinted by the author: one of thefe is an elegy,
as it may be called, upon the death of Sir Philip
Sidney, whom Drayton celebrates as Elphin. It is
to be obferved alfo, that in pofterior impreffions the
arguments preceding the eclogues, and the mottos
by which they are concluded, were omitted." The
fame reafon which has been given by Mr. Collier
for Barnfield's excluding from the new impreffion
the two difputed pieces, namely, that they were not
written by him, might be urged for the rejection of the
" Epitaph upon the Death of his Aunt," or the lines
" Written, at the requeft of a Gentleman, under a Gentlewoman's Picture," and the four other pieces; but
perhaps even he would hardly affert that thefe, any more
than Drayton's omitted pieces, were pirated articles,
and confequently excluded from the new impreffion.
The true explanation of the re-appearance of the two
which are there reprinted feems to be that there exifted
at the end of this volume, after the promife on the title-
page as to the intended contents had been fulfilled, the
whole of one blank page and part of another, which
thefe two pieces could fill up; the " Remembrance of
fome Englifh Poets" therefore conveniently occupies
with its eighteen lines the laft page, and the " Comparifon of the Life of Man," which confifts of only feven
lines, the latter half of the laft page but one. The
felection of the former, which introduces with great
refpect both Shakefpeare, whom he is accufed of robbing
of his Sonnet, and Spenfer, the fubject of it, would
hardly have been made had the author or the publifher
been confcious of fuch a crime; while, curioufly enough,

its fecond line contains the fame epithet applied to Spenfer, namely, " deepe Conceit," which is ufed as a charaċteriſtic of his genius in the difputed fonnet, " In praife of Mufique and Poetrie."

But if the authority of Mr. Collier as a Shakefpearian critic has converted many admirers of our early poetry to his own opinions, others whofe judgment is entitled to refpeċt have not been fo influenced. Among the dif-fentients, Mr. Halliwell, in his folio " Shakefpeare," adheres to the view in favour of Barnfield's claims which he took in the preface to his reprint of " The Affeċtionate Shepheard" for the Percy Society, 1845; and the Rev. W. E. Buckley, an enthufiaſtic ſtudent of our early literature, who was recently fortunate enough to difcover, in the Bodleian, a fecond copy of the fecond edition of Barnfield's poems, 1605, had his previous fuf-picions of the unfoundnefs of Mr. Collier's theory con-firmed by a rigid comparifon of the two impreſſions, with the ufe of which collations I have been favoured for the purpofe of the prefent work, and which would have removed any doubts, if they had exiſted in my mind, of the injuſtice done to Barnfield.

Of Barnfield's life little is known. That he was the fon of a Staffordſhire gentleman, and was born in 1574; that he entered Brazen Nofe College, Ox-ford, in Nov. 1589, and matriculated there, appears from the univerfity records; and alfo, that he took a degree, probably in 1593, is proved by the title-page of his poems. In his " Cynthia," Sonnet IV., he al-ludes to his native county in the line, " As much as Po in clearenes paffeth Trent." He was a member of Gray's Inn, and probably intended for the profeſſion of the law. No mention is made of him by Anthony à Wood, nor has the date of his death been difcovered. But, that he was on good terms with fome of the moft worthy among his contemporaries feems certain, judging from the eulogies, apparently emanating from a warm perfonal feeling, which appear in both editions of his poems, on Spenfer, Daniel, Drayton, and Shakefpeare. So ftrong, indeed, is his veneration for eminent contemporary poets, that, in his earlieft produ&ion, " The Affe&ionate Shepheard," in addition to palpable imitations of them, particularly of the addreffes of Venus to Adonis, he goes out of his way to teftify his regard for Spenfer, Sidney, Fraunce, and Drayton. He is addreffing Love, and fpeaks of thefe friends, under their poetical appel-lations, in the following terms :

> " By thee great Collin loft his libertie,
>   By thee fweet Aftrophel forwent his joy ;
> By thee Amyntas wept inceffantly,
>   By thce good Rowland liv'd in great annoy."

And again, in the fame produ&ion, he alludes, thus feelingly, to his poetical friend, Abraham Fraunce, whofe poem, " The Lamentations of Amyntas for the death of Phillis," dedicated to the Countefs of Pem-broke, to whofe family he was beholden for education and advancement, was publifhed in 1587.

> " And thou, my fweete Amintas, vertuous minde,
>   Should I forget thy learning or thy love,
> Well might l be accounted but unkinde,
>   Whofe pure affe&ion I fo oft did prove,
>   Might my poore plaints hard ftones to pitty move !
> His loffe fhould be lamented of each creature,
> So great his name, fo gentle was his nature."

In the Addrefs to the Reader, in his " Cynthia," he apologizes for it as " the firft imitation of the verfe of that excellent Poet, Maifter *Spencer,* in his *Fayrie Queene.*"

The date of Fraunce's death has not been afcertained; but the above lines prove that it muft have occurred previous to 1594, in which year they firft appeared.

Among the books found at Lamport was a fmall volume, in manufcript, of unpublifhed poetry and profe, evidently the produ&ion of Barnfield, as his name, thus, *Richard Barnfild*, occurs on one of the pages.

## LIST OF EDITIONS.

### I.

THE PASSIONATE Pilgrime. *By W. Shake-fpeare. AT LONDON* Printed for W. Iaggard. and are to be fold by W. Leake, at the Grey-hound in Paules Churchyard. 1599. [16mo. 30 leaves.]

This is fuppofed to be the firft edition. Only two copies are known; one in the Capell colle&ion in Trinity College, Cambridge, which is very dirty from much ufe, and in which the date to the Sonnets is cut off; and the other, bound up with the unique "Venus and Adonis" of 1599, and the "Epigrams and Elegies" of Davies and Marlowe, which was found by the editor in September, 1867, among many precious books of old Englifh poetry, in a lumber-room at Lamport Hall, near Northampton, the feat of Sir Charles Ifham, Bart. This latter is in the cleaneft and moft beautiful condition; and meafures $4\frac{5}{8}$ by $3\frac{1}{8}$ inches.

The Capell copy is bound up with the "Venus and Adonis" of 1620. It was once in the poffeffion of "honeft" Tom Martin of Palgrave, and a MS. note informs us that the volume coft a former owner "but 3 halfpence."

II.

THE PASSIONATE PILGRIME. or *Certaine Amo-rous Sonnets, betweene* Venus *and* Adonis, *newly cor-rected and aug*-mented. *By W. Shakefpere.* The third Edition. Where-unto is newly added two Loue-Epiftles, the firft from *Paris* to *Hellen,* and *Hellens* anfwere backe againe to *Paris.* Printed by W. Iaggard. 1612. [16mo. 62 leaves.]

In the Bodleian copy of this edition Malone has written the following note: "All the poems from Sig. D. 5 were written by Thomas Heywood, who was fo offended at Jaggard for printing them under the name of Shakefpeare, that he has added a poft-fcript to his 'Apology for Actors,' 4to. 1612, on this fubject, and Jaggard, in confequence of it, appears to have printed a new title-page to pleafe Heywood, without the name of Shakefpeare in it. The former title-page was, no doubt, intended to be cancelled, but by fome inadvertence they were both prefixed to this copy, and I have retained them as a curiofity."

The corrected title-page is, except in the ufe of italics and Roman letters, and omitting "*By W. Shakefpere,*" the fame as the firft. This is called "The third Edition," but no other between 1599 and 1612 is known to exift.

III.

POEMS: WRITTEN BY WIL. SHAKE-SPEARE. Gent. Printed at *London* by *Tho. Cotes,* and are to be fold by *Iohn Benfon,* dwelling in St. *Dunftans* Church-yard. 1640. [16mo. Prefixed is a portrait of Shakefpeare by W. Marfhall.]

This confifts of a number of the fonnets, together with fome of the poems from "The Paffionate Pilgrim" and "A Lover's Complaint," as well as fome tranflations from Ovid and other pieces evidently not by Shakefpeare.

IV.

A Collection of Poems, in Two Volumes; Being all
the Miscellanies of Mr. *William Shakespeare,* which
were Publish'd by himself in the year 1609. and now
correctly Printed from those Editions. The First
Volume contains, I. VENUS and ADONIS. II.
The Rape of LUCRECE. III. The Passionate
Pilgrim. IV. Some Sonnets set to sundry Notes of
Musick. The Second Volume contains One Hundred and Fifty Four Sonnets, all of them in Praise
of his Mistress. II. A Lover's Complaint of his
Angry Mistress. *LONDON :* Printed for *Bernard
Lintott,* at the *Cross-Keys,* between the Two Tem-
ple-Gates in *Fleet-street.* [2 vols. fm. 8vo. *circa*
1709.]

The separate title-pages to the pieces in this collection all bear
the same date, 1609, which is that of the first edition of the
Sonnets. But in the Bodleian copy of the first volume the title
pages bear different dates, and are in other respects different. The
copy in the British Museum, in addition to the date of 1709 on
the general title, also bears different ones, that of Venus and
Adonis being 1630; Lucrece, 1632; Passionate Pilgrim, 1599;
Some Sonnets set to Sundry Notes of Musick, 1599.

----

Independent of the general question of the *authorship* of the pieces in "The Passionate Pilgrime," an
interest of another nature attaches to the second part of
it, inasmuch as it is put forth not so much as a literary
work, but as a collection of *sonnets which had been set
to music.* Not only does this fact of poems of such
varied character being so treated illustrate the extent to
which a taste for music was then carried, but it is re-

markable on account of the muſic to all of them, with the exception of two ("My flocks feed not," and " Live with me and be my love") having utterly diſappeared, or at leaſt not being at this time capable of identification. (Oldys, in one of his manuſcripts, ſays they were ſet to muſic by John and Thomas Morley, but he gives no proof of this). And in addition to theſe conſiderations we have to ſeek for an explanation of the meaning of the title itſelf, which, in conſequence of there being no clue to it in the book, is ſufficiently enigmatical to leave us the choice of three hypotheſes; namely, 1. Whether the Muſic was compoſed for Sonnets already written? 2. Whether the Sonnets, like the melodies of Burns and Moore, were written to accompany exiſting Airs? or, 3. Whether the exiſting Sonnets were ſung to Tunes already popular? On a review of the evidence we find proofs of all theſe practices having been adopted.

I. As to the queſtion, Whether it was the cuſtom to compoſe Muſic for Sonnets already written, we find proofs of it in numberleſs publications, among which are thoſe of Byrd, Dowland, Morley, Weelkes (in whoſe collection of Madrigals, dated 1597, "My flocks feed not," firſt appeared), Kirbye, Wilbye, etc., who ſeem to have been indefatigable in procuring and collecting lyric poetry for profeſſional purpoſes.

Another caſe is that of a work entitled "The Teares or Lamentations of a ſorrowfull Soule; by Sir William Leighton, Knight, one of his Majeſties Honourable Band of Gentlemen Penſioners," which was printed in a ſmall volume in 1613; but which the next year appeared in folio, "Compoſed with Muſical Ayres and Songs, both for Voyces and divers Inſtruments. Set

forth by Sir William Leighton," &c. Some of thefe
were fet by John Milton, the father of our great
poet, who, though a fcrivener by profeffion, was a
voluminous and excellent compofer.   And ftill another
example of the fame appears in a work printed
in 1614, entitled, "Ayres made by feverall Authors
and fung in the Mafke at the Marriage of the Right
Honourable Robert Earle of Somerfet, and the Right
Noble Lady Frances Howard.   Set forth to the
Lute and Bafe Violl, and may be expreft by a fingle
voyce to eyther of thofe Inftruments."   [4to. London,
printed for Laurence Lifle.]   Thefe "Ayres" are
fometimes found alone, but more frequently appended
to the "Defcription of a Mafke prefented in the Ban-
quetting roome at Whitehall, etc." [4to. 1614.]   And
as a final illuftration I may mention the "Ayres" of
Alfonfo Ferrabofco [folio; London, printed by T.
Snodham (*alias* T. Efte), for John Brown, 1609], which
contains the mufic to many of Ben Jonfon's Plays and
Mafques.

An additional proof of muficians being in the habit of
adapting mufic to verfes already in exiftence is apparent in the following fact.

In a curious as well as very rare little volume, for it
was unknown both to Hawkins and Burney, entitled, "A
Mufical Banquet, furnifhed with varietie of delicious
Ayres, collected out of the beft Authors; in Englifh,
French, Spanifh, and Italian, by Robert Douland [fon
of the famous John Dowland].   London: Printed for
Thomas Adams, 1610," [folio, and of which a reprint
with the words, "Twenty-five copies only printed"(fmall
8vo. Chifwick Prefs, 1817), was edited by S. W. Singer],
we find fome fpirited and interefting verfes by the un-

fortunate favourite of Elizabeth, the Earl of Eſſex, Sir Philip Sydney, the gallant Earl of Cumberland, Sir Henry Lea, and others unknown. The following is the commencement of Douland's addreſs "To the Reader": "Gentlemen: Finding myſelf not deceived in the hope I had of your kinde entertayning my collection of Lute Leſſons which I lately ſet foorth, I am further encouraged to publiſh unto your cenſure theſe Ayres, being collected and gathered out of the labours of the rareſt and moſt judicious Maiſters of Muſick that either now are or have lately lived in Chriſtendome, whereof ſome I have purpoſely ſorted to the capacitie of young practitioners, the reſt by degrees are of greater depth and ſkill, ſo that like a carefull confectionary, as neere as might be I have fitted my Banquet for all taſtes; if happily [haply] I ſhall be diſtaſted by any, let them know what is brought unto them is dreſt after the Engliſh, French, Spaniſh, & Italian manner," &c. The names of the compoſers are John Douland, Ant. Holborne, R. Martin, R. Hales, D. Batchelar, Teſſeir, Dominico Maria Megli, Giulio Cacciori detto Romano.

II. It is, nevertheleſs, beyond a doubt that Engliſh poets occaſionally wrote words to accompany exiſting muſic, as in the caſe of "Muſica Tranſalpina," in which the Italian Madrigals were tranſlated into Engliſh, and publiſhed by N. Yonge, in 1588; an example followed by the eminent Sonnetteer, Thomas Watſon, in his "Firſt Set of Italian Madrigalls Engliſhed," in which the poetry, though not the muſic, is entirely original. [4to. London, Thomas Eſte, 1590]. It ſeems probable, indeed, from Orlando Gibbons' dedication of his "Firſt Set of Madrigals and Mottets" to Sir

Chriftopher Hatton, dated 1612, that the courtiers of that period fometimes employed themfelves in writing lyrics for their domeftic Lutenifts. One of Watfon's odes bears fo great a refemblance in its commencement to that of Barnfield's poem, " As it fell upon a day," publifhed eight years afterwards, that I cannot refift the temptation of calling attention to it. It is a Birthday Ode to Queen Elizabeth, written probably in the May of 1590 :—

> " This fweet and merry month of May,
>   While nature wantons in her pryme,
> And byrds do fing, and beafts do play,
>   For pleafure of the joyfull time," &c.

A ftill more ftriking inftance of Sonnets being written for exifting mufic is exemplified in a work which is fo rare that only one copy, and that not per-fect, is known to exift, entitled " A Handefull of Plea-fant Delites : Containing Sundrie new Sonets and delectable Hiftories in Diuers Kindes of Meeter. Newly deuifed to the Neweft Tunes, that are now in ufe to be fung. Euery Sonet orderly printed in his proper tune. With New Additions of Certain Songs, to Verie late deuifed Notes, not commonly knowen, nor vfed heretofore. By Clement Robinfon and Diuers Others. At London, Printed by Richard Ihones, dwelling at the figne of the Rofe and Crowne near Holburne Bridge. 1584." [8vo.]

To this volume Dr. Drake, in his " Shakefpeare and his Times," gives high praife. " It is," fays he, " in a great meafure, formed of ballads and fongs, adapted to well-known popular tunes ; and, though its poets have been arbitrarily confined in the ftructure of their verfe by the precompofed mufic, yet many of their lyrics

have a fmoothnefs and fweetnefs in the compofition of
their ftanzas, which may even arreft the attention of
a modern ear. . . . Thirty-two poems occupy
the pages of this pleafing little volume, among which, at
p. 23, is 'A New Courtly Sonet of the Lady Greenfleeves, to the new tune of Greenfleeves,' alluded to by
Shakfpeare in the 'Merry Wives of Windfor,' Act ii.
Sc. 1., and which throws fome curious light on the
female drefs of the period." In addition to Robinfon,
the authors confift of Leonard Gibfon, J. Tomfon, P.
Picks, Thomas Richardfon, and G. Mannington; the
four latter being unknown elfewhere in the annals of
poetry.

Another cafe is that of Anthony Munday, who in
1588 publifhed his " Banqvet of Daintie Conceits; furnifhed with verie delicate and choyfe inuentions, to
delight their mindes, who take pleafure in Mufique,
and there-withall to fing fweete Ditties, either to the
Lute, Bandora, Virginalles, or anie other Inftrument.
Publifhed at the defire of bothe Honorable and Wor-
fhipfull Perfonages, who haue had copies of diuers of
the Ditties heerein contained." Thefe are adapted, as
Munday afferts, to pre-compofed tunes (chiefly popular
dance tunes), and he apologizes for their occafional im-
perfections on account of the difficulty of the tafk. Of
this work only one copy is known.

III. As to the third hypothefis, Whether exifting
Sonnets were fometimes fung to tunes already popular;
we have an important contemporary witnefs to fuch a
practice in William Webbe, who, not confining it to
Ballads only, extends it to the clafs of compofitions found
in " The Paffionate Pilgrime." In his " Difcourfe of
Englifh Poetrie, together with the Author's Judgment

touching the Reformation of our Englifh Verfe," [4to. London, 1586], he fpeaks of "the un-countable rabble of ryminge ballet-makers and compylers of fenfelefs fonnets;" and adds, "there is not anie tune or ftroke which may be fung or plaide on inftruments, which hath not fome poetical ditties framed according to the numbers thereof: fome to 'Rogero,' fome to 'Trenchmore,' to 'Downright Squire,' to galliardes, to pavines, to jygges, to brawles, to all manner of tunes; which every fidler knows better than myfelf, & therefore I will let them paffe." Here the clafs of mufic is named with which old Englifh ditties were ufually coupled—dance and ballad tunes. And it is worthy of remark that, as before mentioned, with the exception of the ode entitled "My flocks feed not," the only piece in "The Paffionate Pilgrime" which has come down to us, of which the mufic is known, is "Live with me and be my love," which being from the fimplicity of its diction fuited to the comprehenfion of the vulgar, became fo popular as to be fung to a common ballad tune.

On a review of all the circumftances, conjoined with the pofitive affertion on the title-page that the Sonnets following had been fet to "Sundry Notes of Mufic," I cannot refift the conclufion that there was once in exiftence an edition in which the Sonnets were accompanied by the mufic, but which, like many other fmall books of that period, has for the prefent, at leaft, difappeared. As a cafe in point, I may mention my finding among the books at Lamport an hitherto unknown edition of Deloney's "Strange Hiftorics," with the mufical notes, dated 1602—the earlieft one previoufly known being 1607; while one, quoted by Percy and Ritfon as of the date of 1612, has hitherto, like an edition printed as early as 1596, or thereabouts, eluded the moſt diligent ſearch. And that this kind of loſs is much greater than is generally ſuppoſed, is illuſtrated again by the library at Lamport, to which we owe the preſervation of more than a dozen works, the very names of which had not previouſly reached us. But that collections of muſic were, from the conſtant uſe to which they were ſubjected, peculiarly liable to deſtruction, is eaſily underſtood, and is proved by the caſe of the ſix following works, (to mention no more), of each of which only a ſingle copy is aſcertained to ſurvive :—

i. "The Cittharn Schoole," by Antony Holborne. [P. Short, 1597; 4to.]

ii. A little tract by John Farmer, entitled "Divers and Sundry waies of two parts in one, to the number of fortie, uppon one playn ſong," etc. [T. Eſte, 1591.]

iii. "Ayres for four Voyces," by Michael Cavendiſh, [P. Short, 1599, folio].

All theſe were till lately utterly unknown, even by name, to muſical hiſtorians and bibliographers.

iv. "Ultimum Vale, or the Third Book of Ayres of 1, 2, 4 Voyces," [folio, London, 1608.]

v. "Private Muſicke," by M. Peerſon, [4to. 1620, in the Douce Collection, Oxford.]

vi. "Varietie of Leſſons: viz. Fantaſies, Pavins, Galliards, Almaines, Corantoes, and Volts," etc. By Robert Dowland : with a Treatiſe on Lute-playing by J. Dowland, [folio, London, 1610.]

The following extracts from Chappell's "Popular Muſic of the Olden Time," ſeem too appropriate to this ſubject to require any apology for their inſertion.

"During the long reign of Elizabeth," he obſerves, "muſic ſeems to have been in univerſal cultivation, as

c

well as in univerfal efteem. Not only was it a neceffary qualification for ladies and gentlemen, but even the city of London advertifed the mufical abilities of boys educated in Bridewell and Chrift's Hofpital, as a mode of recommending them as fervants, apprentices, or hufbandmen. . . . They had mufic at dinner ; mufic at fupper ; mufic at weddings ; mufic at funerals ; mufic at night ; mufic at dawn ; mufic at work ; and mufic at play."

With a tafte for mufic thus generally diffufed among all claffes, both high and low, it might be fuppofed that the number of works, publifhed either as inftructions or as original compofitions, muft have been proportionally great. And that this was fo is plain from the quantity publifhed in England alone during an interval of forty years, between 1589 and 1627, for among thofe which have come down to us are the claffical productions of Byrd, Watfon, Dowland, Efte, Mundy, Yonge, Carlton, Morley, Weelkes, Kirbye, Wilbye, Bennett, Holborne, Farmer, Cavendifh, Pilkington, Robinfon, Batefon, Gibbons, Ward, Hilton and others. Yet amidft all this flood of mufic we feek in vain, with two exceptions, for the notes of mufic to which the Sonnets in " The Paffionate Pilgrime" were fung. But a poffible explanation may be found in the following obfervations of Mr. Chappell in his work already quoted :—

" The fcholaftic mufic of that age," he fays, " great as it was, was fo entirely devoted to harmony, and that harmony fo conftructed upon old fcales, that fcarcely anything like tune could be found in it. . . . . No line of demarcation could be more complete than that between the mufic of the great compofers of the time and what may be termed the mufic of the people.

Perhaps, the only inftance of a tune by a well-known muſician of that age having been afterwards uſed as a ballad tune, is that of ' The Frog Galliard,' compoſed by Dowland. Muſicians held ballads in contempt, and the great poets rarely wrote in ballad metre."

But even with the muſic publiſhed in England our ftock of native growth is not exhauſted, as is proved by the following obſervations of Mr. Chappell, which are of very conſiderable importance as throwing light on the feveral points we have been difcuſſing :—

" We are indebted," he ſays, " to foreign countries for the prefervation of many of the works of our beſt muſicians of this age, as well as of *our popular tunes.* Dr. Bull's muſic is chiefly to be found in foreign manuſcripts, in one of which is ' God fave the King.' Dowland tells us that ' fome part of his poor labours' had been printed in eight cities beyond the feas, viz , Paris, Antwerp, Cologne, Nuremburg, Frankfort, Leipzig, Amſterdam, and Hamburg. Much of the muſic printed in Holland in the feventeenth century was alſo by Engliſh compoſers. The right of printing muſic in England was a monopoly, generally in the hands of one or two muſicians, and therefore very little, and only fuch as they choſe, could be printed. Hence the fcarcity, as well as the frequent imperfection, of thefe early works. This monopoly was held by Tallis and Byrd from 1575 to 1596, then by Morley and his aſſignee."

But a ſimilar monopoly did not extend to the literature, either in manuſcript or in print, of that time, as we fee by the pieces reprinted in the feveral poetical miſcellanies then popular, and in muſical works, the latter of which contain many fonnets and odes written by authors of greater or lefs merit. To the mufical collections of the age of Elizabeth and James, indeed, we are indebted for the prefervation of many moft beautiful fpecimens of lyric poetry not elfewhere to be met with, as well as for the means of completing fome others of which only imperfect verfions had appeared in the poetical mifcellanies of the period; and which, it is highly probable, without the care and accompaniments of fuch enlightened and enthufiaftic profeffors of mufic as thofe already mentioned, would either have never been publifhed, or would have filently difappeared. That thefe compilations were made, generally, without the connivance of the authors is moft probable, as in very few cafes are their names appended. We know to what an extent the practice prevailed in thofe times of poetical compofitions being circulated in manufcript, and as they were not, like mufic, under the protection of the law, it was open to any publifher to appropriate and print them. The "Sonnets" and "Songs" of Shakefpeare in "The Paffionate Pilgrime," the "Epigrammes" of Davies, and other well-known works, are cafes in point.

This opinion, however, of the excellence of the lyric poetry of that age is not fhared by our eminent mufical hiftorian Dr. Burney, who, in his "Hiftory of Mufic," fhows that whatever may be his merits as a mufician, he poffeffed little poetic tafte. "Indeed," he fays, "in more than twenty fets, publifhed between the years 1588 and 1624, including almoft four hundred and fifty Madrigals and Songs in parts, it would be difficult to find any one, of which the words can be perufed with pleafure. The fonnets of Spenfer and Shakfpeare, many of which are worthy of their authors, were indeed not publifhed till about the end of the fixteenth century; but afterwards, it is wonderful that none of them were fet by our beft mufical compofers, except one of Shakfpeare's." And in this concluding obfervation moft readers will concur.

In more recent times, however, according to communications from Mr. A. Roffe, in Notes and Queries, vols. x. and xi., 2nd Ser., two of the Odes, namely, "On a day alack the day," and "Crabbed Age and Youth," have found feveral compofers.

The former (he fays) forms one of the Elegies by Jackfon of Exeter, who has fet it very elegantly for three male voices. It is fet as a folo by T. Chilcot of Bath, about 1750; and as a duet by Sir H. Bifhop. Again, within thefe few years, the poem has been ufed for a prize glee, compofed for four male voices, by W. P. Stevens. In this inftance the compofer omits the laft four lines, and clofes at the words, " That I am forfworn for thee." The laft fix lines of the poem, beginning " Do not call it fin in me," will be found fet as a folo for Lyfander in J. C. Smith's " Fairies"; and thefe fame fix lines have alfo been fet by M. P. King, as a duet for foprano (or tenor) and bafs. This compofition has no accompaniment, and is in the old ftyle of continued imitation between the two voices.

As to the fecond ode; " Crabbed Age and Youth," this (fays Mr. Roffe) has been very beautifully fet by R. J. Stevens as a glee for four male voices, and is a well-known compofition. There are at leaft three other fettings of thefe words: one of thefe, by Signor Giordani, about 1780, is a duet, apparently either for fopranos or tenors; the other two fettings are both by Sir H. Bifhop,— the firft as a fong for Olivia in " Twelfth Night," and the fecond, a totally different compofition, is a dramatic trio for Rofalind, Celia, and Touchftone, and was written for a mufical revival of " As You Like It."

It is fatisfactory to find that the reputation of Dowland, once fo great, ftill furvives. In the " Athenæum" of April, 1868, we read : " A madrigal, by Dowland, was the other day fung at a concert of one of the vocal focieties of Berlin. If we are not miftaken, our Englifh unaccompanied vocal mufic has always ' held its own,' even in the exclufive Sing-Akademie of the Pruffian capital."

And the following extract, relative to Dowland and Shakefpeare, from Mr. J. P. Collier's " Lyrical Poems, felected from Mufical Publications between the years 1589 and 1600," printed for the Percy Society, 1844, feems, for feveral reafons, worthy of a place here :—

" A peculiar intereft attaches to one of the pieces, [' To Cynthia : My thoughts are wing'd with hopes'] in John Dowland's ' Firft Book of Songs' (p. 57), on account of the initials of ' W. S.' being appended to it, in a manufcript of the time preferved in the Hamburgh City Library. It is inferted in ' England's Helicon,' 4to. 1600, as from Dowland's Book of Tablature. without any name or initials; and looking at the character and language of the piece, it is at leaft not impoffible that it was the work of our great dramatift. . . . . If we were to take it for granted, that a fonnet in ' The Paffionate Pilgrim,' 1599, was by Shakefpeare, becaufe it is there attributed to him, we might be fure that he was a warm admirer of Dowland,

> ' whofe heavenly touch
> Upon the lute doth ravifh human fenfe.'

However, it is more than likely, that the fonnet in

which this paſſage is found was by Barnfield, and not by Shakeſpeare : it was printed by Barnfield in 1598, and reprinted by him in 1605, notwithſtanding the intermediate appearance of it in 'The Paſſionate Pilgrim.'"

*THE ISHAM REPRINTS.*

# EPIGRAMMES AND ELEGIES

## BY DAVIES AND MARLOWE.

# EPIGRAMMES:

WRITTEN BY

## SIR JOHN DAVIES;

AND

## CERTAINE OF OVID'S ELEGIES:

TRANSLATED BY

## CHRISTOPHER MARLOWE.

ACCURATELY REPRINTED FROM A RARE EARLY

EDITION IN THE POSSESSION OF

## SIR CHARLES ISHAM, Bart.

WITH A PREFACE

## BY CHARLES EDMONDS,

EDITOR OF THE POETRY OF THE

ANTI-JACOBIN.

## LONDON:

PRINTED AT THE CHISWICK PRESS.

1870.

# EDITOR'S PREFACE.

THESE two fmall works were the production of two noted authors, whofe fame refts upon more enduring foundations than thefe effufions, for the licenfe and coarfenefs of which the only apology that can be made is that they were the outpourings of hot impetuous youth, publifhed in an age when plain fpeaking and indecent ribaldry too often paffed current for wit and mirth. That they poffefs a certain literary value at the prefent day is fhown by their having been thought worthy of re-impreffions by the Rev. A. Dyce and others, and thofe of Davies more recently by the Rev. A. B. Grofart, who has been enabled to include in his complete edition of the works of this author pieces not hitherto publifhed.

The author of the "Epigrammes" became diftinguifhed in after life as a ftatefman, and filled the offices of Solicitor-General and Attorney-General in Ireland, reprefented the boroughs of Corfe Caftle and Newcaftleunder-Lyne, and was Lord Chief Juftice at the time of his death in 1626. The verfatility of his mind is fhown in works of fuch different chara&ers as "Nofce Teipfum," a poem on the nature and immortality of the foul, firft printed in 1599; "Orcheftra," a poem on dancing, firft printed in 1596; in which art he is faid to have been, like another legal dignitary, Sir Chriftopher Hatton, a great proficient; "Hymns of Aftræa," or acroftic verfes in praife of Q. Elizabeth, 1599; a tranflation of the firft fifty pfalms, and other fmaller pieces; while his ability as a political and legal writer is evinced in his "Difcovery of the True Caufes why Ireland was never entirely fubdued," a work of fuch value as to win the high praife of the Earl of Chatham; and in fome profeffional treatifes, which may ftill be referred to with advantage.

Of the "Epigrammes," Mr. Dyce obferves: "Like other colle&ions of the kind which came from the prefs a little later, thefe Epigrams are for the moft part Satires in miniature. They poffefs fome poignancy of ridicule and fome vigour of expreffion, but hardly enough to juftify the applaufes which they once called forth; and they chiefly recommend themfelves to readers of the prefent day as illuftrating the manners and "humours" which prevailed towards the clofe of Elizabeth's reign. When Davies republifhed his Poems in 1622 he did not admit a fingle Epigram into the volume."

The "Elegies" were the juvenile produ&ion of Chriftopher Marlowe, one of the greateft of our dramatic poets, who, after leading a life of great profligacy, met with a violent death, under difgraceful circumftances, in the year 1593, in the thirty-firft year of his age.

Of thefe "Elegies" Mr. Dyce thus fpeaks: "Taken

altogether, this verſion does ſo little credit either to Marlowe's ſkill as a tranſlator or to his ſcholarſhip, that one is
almoſt tempted to believe it was never intended by him
to meet the eye of the world, but was made merely as a
literary exerciſe at an early period of life, when claſſical
ſtudies chiefly engaged his attention. We look in vain
for the graces of Ovid. In many paſſages we ſhould
be utterly puzzled to attach a definite meaning to the
words if we had not the original at hand; and in
many others the Latin is erroneouſly rendered, the
miſtranſlations being ſometimes extremely ludicrous. I
doubt if more can be ſaid in praiſe of this verſion than
that it is occaſionally ſpirited and flowing."

When theſe tracts were publiſhed cannot be aſcertained, none of the editions, of which there were ſeveral,
bearing dates or printers' name. Ritſon believes them
to have been firſt printed in 1596 or 1597. Neither
is it known whether they were iſſued with the connivance of Davies, for as it was the cuſtom in thoſe
days to circulate poems widely in manuſcript before
their appearance in print, and they are mentioned in
Guilpin's "Skialetheia," 1598, where Davies is termed
"our Engliſh Martiall;" in Sir John Harington's "Metamorphoſis of Ajax," 1596; in Baſtard's "Chreſtoleros,"
1598, &c., and they all bear his initials I. D.; the
author's name could have been no ſecret. Shakeſpeare's
"Venus and Adonis," it may be remarked, was noticed
by Lodge in his "Scillaes Metamorphoſis," in 1589,
which was four years before its public appearance in
print. But there were perfectly obvious reaſons why
he would not like to openly avow himſelf the author
of pieces, which, though they might increaſe his reputation for wit and humour, would be conſidered as highly

indecorous in a young and rifing barrifter. It is figni-
ficant that when he brought out a new edition of his
Poems a few years before his death the Epigrammes
were omitted. What was thought of them by the
authorities was fhown by that memorable event in the
annals of literature when, to ufe the words of Warton,
in his Hiftory of Englifh Poetry, "in the year 1599 the
Hall of the Stationers underwent as great a purgation
as was carried on in Don Quixote's library. Marfton's
' Pygmalion,' Marlowe's ' Ovid,' the 'Satires of Hall
and Marfton,' the 'Epigrams' of Davies and others,
and the 'Caltha Poetarum,' were ordered for immediate conflagration by the prelates Whitgift and
Bancroft," together with other works, that of Guilpin's,
named above, being one. Notwithftanding this inter-
diction, feveral editions of both works were fecretly
printed, all of which, in confequence of the hafty and
furreptitious manner in which they were prepared,
abound with the groffeft errors.

## LIST OF EDITIONS.

### I.

EPIGRAMMES AND ELEGIES. By I. D. and
C. M. At Middleborough [n. d. 12mo. A—G 3,
in fours. 26 leaves.]—[*Sir C. Ifham.*]

This is the edition now reprinted, and though for reafons hereafter given it is not in my opinion the very earlieft impreffion, yet
to judge merely from its containing, like the one next to be defcribed, only "Certaine of Ovids Elegies," it muft have preceded
all thofe which include the whole of his Three Books. Notwithftanding its imprint of *Middleborough*, there is as much probability,

if the character of the type and of the mifprints be evidence, that it iffued from the fame prefs as "The Paffionate Pilgrime," and confequently a London one, as that the edition next defcribed was printed abroad and by foreigners.

## II.

## EPIGRAMMES AND ELEGIES. By I. D. and C. M. At Middleborugh; [no date, duodecimo. A. 2 leaves. B—C in fours].—[*Britiſh Muſeum*].

This copy is deficient of one leaf (A 4), and was fold at Bindley's fale for £8 18*s*. 6*d*. It bears the following autograph note by that eminent collector: "This is the original and genuine edition: of extreme rarity ; printed abroad, and uncaftrated."

This opinion is, I think, only partially correct. That the Bindley impreffion was printed abroad is unqueftionable, but inftead of the works firft iffuing from a foreign prefs, I believe that we owe them to a London one ; for their groffnefs, though occafionally remarkable, not being greater than that which characterifes many other works then openly circulated, they would not be likely, in the opinion of the putters-forth, to incur the cenfure of the authorities, and therefore no neceffity would exift for their being printed elfewhere than in the metropolis. When, to cite only one example, it was feen that Sir John Harington's tranflation of the "Orlando Furiofo," 1596, though disfigured occafionally by fuch unneceffary groffnefs as would have fhocked Ariofto himfelf, had been produced under the fpecial fanction of the "maiden queen," and was never interfered with, it might be difficult for publifhers to guefs what would be fufficiently licentious to bring down upon them the cenfure of the Church. And therefore I think that it was only fubfequent to their original publication in London, and in confequence of their being included among the books burnt at Stationers' Hall in June, 1599, that the expedient of reprinting thefe Epigrammes and Elegies at Middleburgh, in Holland, was firft reforted to.

That no copy with a *London* imprint is known to exift militates nothing againft this fuppofition, my recent difcovery of fo many hitherto unknown editions as well as works encouraging us to hope for future refufcitations of books of equal or even greater importance.

## III.

## ALL OVID'S ELEGIES: 3 Bookes. By C. M. EPIGRAMS by J. D. At Middlebourgh ; [n. d. 12mo. A—F, in eights, including title.] [48 leaves].

"A later edition, which I have ufed, and which contains the 'Elegies' complete, with their more objectionable paffages rather heightened than foftened down, is probably that which was burnt at Stationers' Hall by order of the Archbifhop of Canterbury and the Bifhop of London, in June, 1599." Dyce; who refers to it as edition B. A duplicate verfion of Eleg. XV. lib. i. is afcribed to B. J., probably Ben Jonfon, and if fo, it muft have been his earlieft printed production.

## IV.

## ALL OVID'S ELEGIES; 3 Bookes. By C. M. EPIGRAMS by J. D. At Middlebovrgh ; [n. d. 12mo.] [Referred to by Mr. Dyce as ed. C.]

Editions of the two works continued to be printed together, with *Middleburgh* on the title, and without date, but probably in London, as late as 1640. As to recent impreffions, both were included by the Rev. A. Dyce, in his editions of "Marlowe's Works," in 1850 and 1865 ; and Mr. G. Robinfon, in his edition of "Marlowe's Works," 3 vols. Pickering, 1826, has likewife inferted the "Epigrammes" and both verfions of the "Elegies." The "Epigrammes" alfo appear in the new edition of the "Complete Works of Sir John Davies," now in courfe of publication by the Rev. A. B. Grofart. An edition of the "Certaine" impreffion of the Elegies, limited to twenty-five copies, was printed a few years fince, without date, by Mr. Maitland.

The "Middleburgh" here mentioned is the capital of the Ifle of Walcheren, the firft incorporated city of Holland and Zealand that ever exifted, and once of confiderable importance to Englifh commerce, as enjoying the excluſive right of depofit for the cloths imported from London. Chaucer, in defcribing the Merchant in the Canterbury Tales, alludes to the conftant traffic "Betwixen Middleburgh and Oréwell," and Caxton is fuppofed to have had an agency here. It is alfo the city in which the telefcope was invented. On its capture from the Spaniards by the Dutch in 1574 they immediately abolifhed the Roman Catholic worfhip and efta-blifhed a free prefs. In confequence it feems to have been felected as a convenient place for printing various Englifh books which might have met with oppofition from the authorities in England. As early as 1582 Robert Brown's "Lives of all True Chriftians," of which a copy is preferved in Trinity College, Dublin, was printed here, as alfo were feveral other Englifh books before the clofe of the fixteenth century; among them Dudley Fenner's "Song of Songs," and fome pieces of that extraordinary character, Hugh Broughton. In 1584 R. Schilders, who ftyles himfelf printer to the States of Zealand, publifhed here a Dutch tranflation of Lord Burleigh's celebrated tract "On the Execution of Juftice in England," &c., which had firft appeared about 1578; and in 1599 an edition of John Rainolde's "Overthrow of Stage Playes," fome copies of which bear the date of 1600.

*Now Ready.* *An accurate re-impreſſion, printed for the Subſcribers only, of the following intereſting work, of which only two copies are known :*

# Newes out of Powles Churchyarde.

Now newly renued and amplifyed according to the accidents of the preſent time, 1579, and other-wiſe entituled ſyr Nummus. Written in Engliſh Satyrs. Wherein is reprooved exceſſiue and un-lawfull ſeeking after riches, and the euill ſpending of the ſame. Compyled by E. H. Gent.
Imprinted at London by John Charlewood, and Richard Jhones. [8vo. Black Letter.]

\**\* The impreſſion of this work is ſtrictly limited to One Hundred and Twenty-nine Copies, namely :

One Hundred on Small Paper, price 10s. 6d. each.
Twenty-five on Large Paper, price 21s.
Four on Vellum, two of which are of the Larger Size.

This curious and exceſſively rare poetical work, by EDWARD HAKE, was found by the editor at Lamport Hall on the ſame occaſion, in September, 1867, as brought to light the hitherto unknown edition of " Shakeſpeare's Venus and Adonis," dated 1599, as well as many other rare and undeſcribed productions of the Elizabethan era. *Till then only one copy was ſup-poſed to be in exiſtence.*

Its *Rarity,* however, is not its only recommendation, for it throws much light on the manners and cuſtoms of the time. It conſiſts of a ſpirited dialogue (in eight Satyrs, as they are called,) between Bertulph and Paul as they walk in the aifle of St. Paul's Cathedral, then a favourite refort both for bufinefs and pleafure. The author, who was Under Steward of Windfor, and a dependant of the great Earl of Leicefter, to whom he dedicates this work, inveighs with much feverity on the abufes in all branches of fociety, attacking the rapacity and idlenefs of Church dignitaries, the corruption and partiality of judges and the greedinefs of counfel and attorneys; the tricks and practifes of phyficians, apothecaries and furgeons; the unneceffary extravagance of living and confequent ruin of thoughtlefs perfons; the wickednefs of bawds, ufurers, brokers, &c., and introducing allufions to unlawful fports, the fumptuary laws then in force, &c.

Of its claims to notice Mr. Payne Collier thus fpeaks in his recently publifhed "Bibliographical and Critical Account of the rareft Books in the Englifh Language" :—

" There is no more rare or more curious work than this in our language. Only a fingle copy of it is known (that we have ufed); and, although mentioned by later bibliographers, it was unknown to Ritfon, and nobody has yet pretended to give a notion of its contents. We fhall do fo in more detail than ufual." And to this purpofe he devotes no lefs than fix pages.

*.* *Subfcribers' names can be fent to the publifhers, Meffrs. H. Sotheran & Co., 136, Strand, London; or to the editor, Mr. Charles Edmonds (Sackett and Edmonds), 11, Bull Street, Birmingham.*

the exception of the date, &c. Minute differences alfo exift in the text, which prove them to be diftinct impreffions.

It is a tolerably printed and very rare edition. Though Hibbert's copy produced only £1 14s. by public auction in 1829, one was purchafed at Sotheby's in May, 1856, for £49 10s. by Mr. H. Stevens, at whofe fale, in Auguft, 1857, it brought the fum of £56, having then been bound in morocco by Bedford.

Hibbert's copy, now in the Britifh Mufeum, bears the appearance of having been well read : it is ftained, and a few leaves are mended, but generally it is in good condition. It meafures 4¼ by 3⅞ inches, and is bound in ruffia.

XIII.

# VENVS AND ADONIS. 1675. [8vo.]

In the Bodleian catalogue, fays the Cambridge editor, a copy is mentioned of the date 1675, but none fuch exifts in the library itfelf. It may be the edition defcribed by Mr. Halliwell as "a chap-book impreffion, 'Printed by Elizabeth Hodgkinfonne, for F. Coles, T. Vere, J. Wright, and J. Clark,' a quaint-looking diminutive volume of extreme rarity." According to Bohn's Lowndes, a copy was fold at Naffau's fale, in 1824, bound in ruffia, for £2 5s.

Some time previous to the year 1655, the copyright paffed into the hands of Edward Wright, who affigned it to William Gilbertfon, the 4th April, 1655. No edition, however, between thofe of 1636 and 1675 is known to have furvived, which ftrengthens my opinion already expreffed that feveral impreffions have difappeared without " leaving a wrack behind."

obferves, "Another edition is faid to have appeared at London in
1630, the only authority for which is a ftatement in fome copies
of Lintot's reprints of 1711, copies of thofe reprints varying in the
feparate titles, that he copied the Venus and Adonis from an
edition printed at London in 1630."

The title-page, including the figure of a Cupid, fo exactly
refembles that in the impreffion of 1636 by the fame printer, with
the exception of the date, which is unequivocally 1630, that at
firft fight the date and the initials of the printer, which are J. H.
inftead of I. H., might be confidered mifprints, but a comparative
examination of the two books proves them to be diftinct editions.
The text alfo differs in various places from that of the copy with
manufcript title-page mentioned below.

This volume meafures 4⅝ by 3⁵⁄₁₀ inches.

### XI.

VENVS AND ADONIS. *Vilia miretur vulgus, &c.*
[Small 8vo.   27 leaves.]   (1630?)

In the Bodleian Library is an edition wanting the printed title-
page, which has been fupplied by one in manufcript, purporting
that the book was printed in London in the year 1630, and it has
accordingly been catalogued as if printed in that year.   It might
have been fuppofed that this is identical with the recently-difcovered
edition of 1630, but Mr. Harper, on comparing them, finds them
to be different impreffions.

"Whatever be the true date," fays the Rev. W. G. Clark (who
was not aware, when he printed the invaluable Cambridge Shakefpeare in 1866, of the exiftence of the edition of *Coules*, 1630),
it is certainly earlier than that of Coules, 1636."

This volume meafures 4¹¹⁄₁₀ by 2⁵⁄₁₀ inches.

### XII.

VENVS *AND* ADONIS. *Vilia miretur vulgus, &c.*
LONDON, Printed by I. H. and are to be fold by
*Francis Coules* in the *Old Baily* without Newgate.
1636. [Sm. 8vo.   27 leaves.]

The title-page of this edition bears fome refemblance to that
dated 1630 by the fame printer, defcribed by me as No. X., with

## IX.

**VENVS AND ADONIS.** *Vilia miretur vulgus, &c.*
*EDINBVRGH,* Printed by *Iohn Wreittoun,* and
are to bee fold in his Shop a litle be-*neath the Salt
Trone.* 1627. [Small 8vo. 22 leaves.]

Of this edition only two copies are known, one of which is preferved in the Britifh Mufeum. The Cambridge editor " believes
that it was printed frcm a manufcript which the writer had copied
from the Bodleian copy of the impreffion of 1602, but in which he
had introduced, probably by happy conjecture, feveral emendations
agreeing with the text of the three earlieft editions." Beloe, in his
" Anecdotes of Literature," erroneoufly gives the date as 1607.

The Mufeum copy belonged to George Chalmers, at whofe
fale in March, 1842, it was purchafed by Mr. B. H. Bright for
£37 10s. At the latter's fale, in 1845, it was fecured by the
Britifh Mufeum for the fum of £35. Its fhape is peculiar, being
an elongated fmall 8vo. meafuring 5 5/16 by 3½ inches. The title-
page is mounted and a few leaves are mended. Page 13 is mifprinted ; 32 is mifprinted 23 ; and the laft page, 46, is mifprinted
47. It has Geo. Chalmers's book-plate, and is bound in modern
calf.

The other copy, which, ftrange to fay, is in an uncut ftate, was
fold at Sotheby's, in 1864, for £115. It had been found by a
country bookfeller in a lot of worthlefs books at a fale.

## x.

**VENVS *AND* ADONIS** *Vilia miretur vulgus, &c.*
LONDON, Printed by J. H. and are to be fold by
*Francis Coules* in the *Old Baily* without Newgate
1630. [Small 8vo. 27 leaves.]

This is apparently an unique copy of a hitherto doubtiul edition,
preferved among Anthony à Wood's books, which were recently
removed from the Afhmolean Mufeum to the Bodleian Library.
It was difcovered by Mr. H. S. Harper, to whom I am indebted
for an account of it.

The tradition that an edition had been really printed in 1630, was
therefore founded on fact. Mr. Halliwell, in his folio Shakefpeare,

fold for more than £40. George Daniel. Canonbury." The fact, however, is that at Bindley's fale in 1819 it was purchafed by Mr. Strettell for £42; and at his fale in 1841 it was bought in for £26 5s., and afterwards fold for £40 to Mr. Daniel, who parted with it to the Britifh Mufeum.

The Bodleian copy meafures $5\frac{9}{16}$ by $3\frac{3}{8}$ inches. Another is preferved at Shirburn Caftle, Oxfordfhire, the feat of the Earl of Macclesfield.

### VII.

VENUS *AND* ADONIS. *Vilia miretur vulgus, &c.* *LONDON*, Printed for *W.B.* 1617. [Small 8vo. 27 leaves.]

" A copy of this edition," fays Bohn's Lowndes, " is in the Bodleian Library. (Mr. Dyce mentions an edition of 1616, but he is the only authority for it.)" It would appear from Lowndes that no copy has been fold by auction; a proof of its extreme rarity. In March, 1620, William Barrett affigned the copyright to John Parker.

### VIII.

VENVS AND ADONIS. *Vilia miretur vulgus, &c.* *LONDON*, Printed for *I.P.* 1620. [Small 8vo. 27 leaves.]

Of this edition, of which Lowndes cannot indicate the fale of a fingle copy, the Cambridge editor fays, " A copy exifts in the Capell collection. Dr. Bandinel alfo purchafed one for the Bodleian, but it cannot now be found."

The Capell copy is bound up with " The Paffionate Pilgrime " of 1599; and formerly belonged to the antiquary, Tom Martin, of Palgrave, the hiftorian of Thetford, whofe autograph it bears. A previous poffeffor purchafed the volume for three halfpence. It meafures $4\frac{1}{2}$ by $3\frac{1}{4}$ inches.

John Parker held the copyright until May 7, 1626, when he parted with it to John Haviland and John Wright, fen.

diſtinct impreſſions were made, of each of which only a ſingle copy exiſts; one preſerved in the Britiſh Muſeum, and the other in the Bodleian Library. I will give the account of them in his own words.

"The imprint of the former is as follows:

> "Imprinted at London for *William Leake*,
> "dwelling at the ſigne of the Holy Ghoſt, in
> "Paules Church-yard. 1602."

"The title-page of the Bodleian copy is the ſame as that of the Muſeum copy, excepting that it has '*vulgus: mibi*' for '*vulgus, mihi*,' and 'Pauls Churchyard' for 'Paules Church-yard,' and the printer's device is different.   The ſimilarity of title-page and identity of date have led to the ſuppoſition that theſe were copies of the ſame edition, but a compariſon of the two proves to demonſtration that they were different editions.   The Bodleian copy is very inferior to the Muſeum copy in typography, in the quality of the paper, and in accuracy.   The Muſeum copy formerly belonged to the late Mr. George Daniel, who has written in a fly-leaf the following note: 'No other copy of this exceſſively rare edition is known.   Mr. Evans was wrong in ſtating that a copy is in the Malone Collection in the Bodleian Library.   No copy is mentioned in the catalogue, nor is there one to be found there.'   Mr. Daniel had overlooked the exiſtence of the Bodleian copy of 1602; but, as it turns out, his own copy is unique after all.   That in the Bodleian has the autograph of R. Burton, author of the "Anatomy of Melancholy."   Neither was printed from the other, but both from the ſuppoſititious edition of 1600."

The copy in the Britiſh Muſeum meaſures $5\frac{3}{16}$ by $3\frac{1}{8}$ inches.   It was formerly George Steevens's, and has, in addition to a MS. note on the baſe of the title-page, the following in his handwriting, together with others by Mr. Jas. Bindley and Mr. G. Daniel.   It is printed on thick paper, and is in good condition, with the exception of four leaves, which are mended, and is bound in yellow morocco.

"Bought at the Auction of Dr. Chauncy's library April 15. 1790. 1745. for 0 8s. 0d.   Of this edition of Shakſpeare's Venus & Adonis I have met with no other copy.   G. S."   "Bought at Mr. Steevens's Sale, May 21ſt, 1800 for £1 11s. 6d, No. 1361. J E."   "Bought at Mr. Strettle's Sale 13 May 1841 at Evans's: Lot 350: for £40 8s 6d.   At Mr. Bindley's Sale this Copy was

powerful enemies, and written by a poet, who though protected by popular favour and by admirers in high places, must have offended the foes of Effex by his loudly proclaimed praife. Thefe are mere conjectures, but everything connected with our bard is fo interefting that no fact at all bearing upon his works fhould pafs unnoticed even though it be put forth by fo humble a worker and admirer as the penner of the prefent lines.

V.

## VENVS AND ADONIS. (1600?)

In the Bodleian Library is an edition in fmall 8vo. with a manu-fcript title-page, purporting that the volume was "printed by I. H. for Iohn Harrifon. 1600." This date, as mentioned in the preceding article, was probably felected on account of this im-preffion being bound up with the "Lucrece" of that year. But Mr. Halliwell, in his folio Shakefpeare, had already pointed out that no edition of 1600 with fuch an imprint could have exifted, for Harifon had affigned the copyright to Leake four years previoufly.

"This edition," fays the Cambridge editor (the Rev. W. G. Clark), "was printed from that of 1596," a conclufion from which I prefume to differ. From a comparifon of the two, I am of opinion that the newly difcovered edition of 1599 is copied from the impreffion of 1596, and is prior to the one in queftion. The firft four editions generally agree, but with this impreffion of 1600 begins a frefh feries of readings, which are copied in the fubfequent ones; a fact confirmed by the Cambridge editor, as he fays, "It contains many erroneous readings, due, it would feem, partly to carelefnefs and partly to wilful alteration, which were repeated in later copies."

This volume meafures $4\frac{8}{16}$ by $2\frac{11}{16}$ inches, and contains 27 leaves, as do the other editions.

VI.

*VENVS* AND ADONIS. *Vilia miretur vulgus, &c.* Imprinted at London for *William Leake*, dwelling at the figne of the Holy Ghoft, in Paules Church-yard. 1602. [Sm. 8vo. 27 leaves.]

Of this edition it has been difcovered by one of the editors of the "Cambridge Shakefpeare," (the Rev. W. G. Clark), that two

b

eyes of a sovereign who was unreasonably jealous of any free-will in matrimonial matters on the part of her favourite courtiers. But in this case the royal displeasure was aggravated by the ill-judged conduct of Lord Essex who, instead of realizing the expectations of his friends in his conduct of the expedition against the Irish rebels, came back dishonoured. In the chorus to the fifth act of " Henry V." Shakespeare, the friend of both Essex and Southampton, thus anticipates his triumphant return :—

> " But now behold,
> In the quick forge and working house of thought,
> How London doth pour out her citizens!
> The mayor, and all his brethren, in best sort,—
> Like to the senators of the antique Rome,
> With the plebeians swarming at their heels,—
> Go forth, and fetch their conquering Cæsar in :
> As, by a lower, but by loving likelihood,
> Were now the general of our gracious empress
> (As, in good time, he may) from Ireland coming,
> Bringing rebellion broached on his sword,
> How many would the peaceful city quit
> To welcome him?"

But his reception was very different! His unauthorized truce with those he had been sent to subdue and his unexpected return from Ireland, brought down upon himself the censures of the court, and what was worse, those of a sovereign then surrounded by his personal enemies. Southampton was peremptorily dismissed by Elizabeth from the command to which Essex had appointed him in that country, and he felt no inclination to show himself at court. It was at this period, as appears by a letter from Rowland Whyte to Sir Robert Sydney, preserved in the Sydney Papers, that " My Lord Southampton and Lord Rutland came not to the court ; the one doth but very seldom : they pass away the time in London merely in going to plays every day." Rutland also was connected with Essex by family ties, having married the daughter of Lady Essex by her first husband, the accomplished Sir Philip Sydney.

Under these untoward circumstances, it is possible that a printer might deem it advisable to defer publishing a work which, though licensed some years before, had always been viewed with ungracious eyes by the dispensers of authority; which was dedicated to a conspicuous courtier now under a cloud and exposed to the malice of

directed " to bee called in." But this fame order reveals two other important facts, the firft of which is that among other arbitrary powers granted by the aforenamed decree of the Star Chamber, of 23rd June, 1585, the Privy Council, reprefented by the Archbifhop of Canterbury and the Bifhop of London, claimed the abfolute right not only of feizing any book they chofe, even after its having been licenfed, but of prohibiting its reprint altogether, as in the cafe of the works of Tom Nafh and Gabriel Harvey, all of which were to " be taken wherefoever they maye be found, and none of theire bookes bee ever printed hereafter." The fecond relates to a prac- tice we fhould have little fufpected, namely, the obtaining of licenfes to print under falfe pretences. This is plainly evidenced by the following claufe in the faid order: "That thoughe any booke of the nature of theife heretofore expreffed fhalbe broughte unto you under the hands of the Lo. Archebifshop of Canter- burye, or the Lo. B. of London, that the faid booke fhall not bee printed untill the Mr. or wardens have acquainted the faid Lo. Arp. or the Lo. B. with the fame to knowe whether it be theire hand or no."

Without, however, laying any ftrefs on the probability of this or any other edition of "Venus and Adonis" having been feized for its licentioufnefs, we have reafon from other fources to fuppofe it was never favourably regarded by the ecclefiaftical authorities, although they had duly licenfed it. But it had been brought out under the protection of a powerful patron, who was then a favourite at court : no flight advantage in thofe times ; as is hinted at in his "Account of Marlowe and his Writings," by Mr. Dyce, who fays, "We may wonder at the inconfiftency of the book-inquifitors of thofe days, who condemned to the flames Marlowe's 'Ovid's Elegies,' Marfton's 'Metamorphofis of Pyg- malion's Image,' nay, even Hall's 'Satires,' and yet fpared Har- ington's 'Orlando Furiofo,' which equals the original in licentiouf- nefs, and is occafionally fo grofs in expreffion that it would have fhocked Ariofto. The truth may be, that 'the authorities' did not choofe to meddle with a tranflation which was not only dedicated to the Virgin Queen, but had been executed at her defire."

But curioufly enough in this fame year, 1599, it was the mif- fortune of Lord Southampton to feel the ftings of court difgrace. He had married the year previoufly, without the confent of the Queen, Elizabeth Vernon, a coufin of Lord Effex. Under any circumftances this would have been a grave offence in the

of that of 1602 only two ; of the Edinburgh edition by John Wreittoun, 1627, only two ; and when we reflect that of many other popular contemporary works not one copy is now known to exift, there is nothing unreafonable in the fuppofition that more editions of the "Venus and Adonis,"—a poem of all others which would be read with avidity both by the learned and the unlearned, and confequently more liable to fpeedy deftruction—were printed than has been hitherto fufpected.

For the difappearance of fo many works obvious reafons may be affigned, fuch as their popularity among all claffes, their continual ufe, and the natural careleffnefs of common readers, the limited number printed, and their fmall fize ; while the copies in the pof-feffion of a higher order of fociety no doubt fhared the fate of many other valuable objects in the Fire of London, the Civil Wars, etc.

But another caufe was likewife in operation, and this was the frequent feizure of books by the Privy Council. The power of the court in thofe days to inflict vengeance on its victims was evidenced in various ways, and in printing and publifhing matters was provided by that moft arbitrary decree of the Star Chamber, dated 23rd June, 1585, which in addition to other regulations, gave unlimited authority to the ecclefiaftical authorities to feize and deftroy whatever books they thought proper. A notable inftance of this interference with books already printed took place in this very year, 1599, at Stationers' Hall, when a number of objectionable works were condemned to the flames, and fpecial admonitions given then and there to the printers, among whom were fome of the moft eminent of the time, including Adam Iflip, Edmund Bollifant, Valentine Simmes, John Windet, Richard Field, the original printer of the "Venus and Adonis," and others.

Although only one fuch comprehenfive literary *auto da fè* is recorded, feizures of books fo conftantly took place, that the authorities would think it unneceffary to regifter them, and the difficulty of arriving at the truth of even recorded facts is illuftrated by the circumftance that Warton and his copyifts uniformly affert that in the aforefaid conflagration Hall's "Satires" and Cutwode's "Caltha Poetarum" were included; but in the "Order" for this burning, figned by Archbifhop Whitgift and Bifhop Bancroft, preferved in Stationers' Hall, and which I for the firft time printed verbatim, in "Notes and Queries," 3rd Ser. vol. xii. it is expreffly ftated that thefe two works were reprieved ("ftaid"); and Willobie's "Avifa," not previoufly included in the warrant, was

Not only does a comparative examination prove that thefe are different impreffions, but as the text of this edition of 1599 agrees generally with that of 1596, it may reafonably be fuppofed that the former preceded the edition with the prefumed date of 1600.

On the difcovery of this edition, a limited reprint was fuggefted for the purpofe of perpetuating a curiofity in literature; and as the great intereft confifts in an accurate reproduction of the text as it appears in the volume, the moft fcrupulous pains have been taken by the editor to prevent any deviation from the original; confequently no attempts have been made to correct even palpable errors. The type has been imitated as clofely as poffible, and occupies the fame length of page as in the original; while the title-page, ornamental letters, and head and tail-pieces, have been cut in fac-fimile.

Though this poem achieved fuch fudden popularity that the edition of 1593 was fucceeded by another early in 1594, we know of no re-impreffion till that of 1596; but it is hardly likely that the new proprietor, John Harifon, was not called upon for a new one before this. Early in the latter year he publifhed what was doubtlefs intended as a popular edition, in fmall octavo fize, the previous ones being in quarto; and then, after having poffeffed the copyright only two years, he difpofed of it to William Leake, who, according to prefent appearances, produced no edition till three years afterwards, in 1599, and the fame interval elapfed before his edition of 1602 was publifhed. I lay no ftrefs on the fuppofititious edition of 1600, for this was evidently, from the ftate of the text, fubfequent to that of 1599. But the moft remarkable circumftance is that no editions between thofe of 1602 and 1617, at which latter date Leake parted with the copyright to William Barrett, are known to exift.

There are grounds, therefore, for believing that feveral editions of this poem difappeared foon after the firft publication of it. It is fcarcely poffible that impreffions of a work of fuch fplendour, and fo fuited to the public tafte—fo fuperior to every production of the kind that had preceded it—in fact, a work that had created in the minds of readers a new fenfation—fhould not have followed each other with greater rapidity than would be evidenced by the few which have come down to our time. When we confider that of the firft edition only one copy has furvived; of the fecond only three; of that of 1596 only two; of our prefent edition only one; of the fuppofititious edition of 1600 only one;

Daniel for £91 10s. At the fale of the library of this latter diftinguifhed collector, in 1864, it was fecured by the Britifh Mufeum
for the fum of £336. In the beginning of the volume is a
manufcript note from the eminent bookfeller, Thomas Rodd,
written in the auction-room during the fale, warning Mr. Daniel that
there was no likelihood of his obtaining it under £100 : alfo another in the handwriting of Mr. Daniel.

IV.

# VENVS AND ADONIS. *Vilia miretur vulgus, &c.* Imprinted at London for William Leake, dwelling in Paules Churchyard at the figne of the Greyhound. 1599. [Sm. 8vo. 27 leaves.]

A HITHERTO-UNDESCRIBED EDITION, AND FROM THE ONLY COPY
OF IT KNOWN TO EXIST, THE PRESENT REPRINT HAS BEEN MADE.
It is, confequently, in every fenfe of the word, UNIQUE.

This moft precious volume I had the good fortune to difcover
in a lumber-room at Lamport Hall, Northamptonfhire, the feat
of Sir Charles'Ifham, Bart. in September, 1867. Bound in the
fame vellum cover, are "The Paffionate Pilgrime," of the fame
date; prefumed to be the firft edition, and of which only one
other copy is known; and the fuppreffed "Epigrammes and Elegies"
of Davies and Marlowe, and the latter's verfions of "Ovid's
Elegies;" all of which I have likewife reprinted. The volume
throughout is wonderfully clean and frefh, bound in the wrapping
vellum of the period, with ftrings, and with no outward indication
of its contents. It meafures 4⅝ by 3⅛ inches.

The text is evidently a copy of that of previous editions; but
while a few corrections are introduced, they bear no proportion to
the mifprints, which are fuch as could have arifen only from the
abfence of that indifpenfable fupervifion which is now exercifed
by the corrector of the prefs. When this edition was difcovered,
it was imagined that it might be identical with the one mentioned
below (No. V.), preferved in the Bodleian, which, being without
a title-page, had had attached to it the fuppofititious date of
1600, in confequence of its being bound up with the unique
copy of the "Lucrece" of that date, "printed by I. H. for
Iohn Harrifon," which had been given by Dr. Farmer to Malone.

This impreffion was unknown to Malone, who erroneoufly fuppofed that of 1596 to be the fecond edition. In Mr. Davies' valuable "Memoir of the York Prefs," (1 vol. 8vo. Nichols, 1868) it is ftated that in the catalogue of the books belonging to John Fofter, bookfeller there, who died in 1616, an edition of the "Venus and Adonis" is valued at *threepence*, and "The Paffionate Pilgrime," at *fivepence:* unfortunately to neither of thefe items is the date of the edition attached.

Only three copies of this edition are known—I. The one in the Grenville collection in the Britifh Mufeum, which formerly belonged to the eminent collector, Mr. Jolley, who had purchafed it in Lancafhire for a mere trifle: unfortunately it is cut clofe and mended. It meafures $6\frac{3}{16}$ by $4\frac{7}{8}$ in., and is richly bound in olive morocco. It realized at his fale in 1844 the fum of £116. II. Mr. H. Huth's, a fair copy, very fuperior to the preceding one, meafuring $7\frac{1}{4}$ by $4\frac{13}{16}$ in. It formerly belonged to Mr. G. Daniel, at whofe fale, in 1864, it produced £240. III. The copy in the Bodleian Library, bequeathed by Mr. Caldecott, meafuring $6\frac{3}{4}$ by $4\frac{3}{8}$ in.

### III.

### VENVS AND ADONIS. *Vilia miretur vulgus, &c.* Imprinted at London by R. F. for Iohn Harifon, 1596. [Sm. 8vo. 27 leaves.]

This edition, like the preceding ones, iffued from the prefs of Richard Field, who, though he had parted with his property in it, was ftill employed to print it. It bears his device of the anchor, but a fmaller and lefs elaborately executed one than that on the "Lucrece" of 1594. It muft have been publifhed early in the year 1596, for Harifon transferred the copyright to Leake in June, after having poffeffed it only two years. The text clofely follows that of the preceding impreffion. I have noticed, however, at leaft a dozen frefh errors; but there are, on the other hand, a few alterations, which are fometimes improvements—both of which changes are doubtlefs due to the printer.

Only two copies are known—I. The one in the Malone collection in the Bodleian Library, meafuring $4\frac{1}{4}$ by 3 inches. The other, which is a very fine one, meafuring $4\frac{7}{8}$ inches, and half bound, after being fold at Mr. Bolland's fale at Evans's in 1840, for £91, to Mr. B. H. Bright, was purchafed at his fale in 1845, by Mr. G.

II.

## VENVS AND ADONIS. *Vilia miretur vulgus, &c.* 1594.

The Second Edition, alfo in quarto, confifting of the fame number of leaves as the Firft, and likewife printed by Richard Field. The title-page alfo is exactly fimilar, except in the alteration of the date.

This edition "followed hard upon" the preceding one, for it muft have been printed early in 1594, as the transfer of the copyright from Field to Harifon is recorded at Stationers' Hall as having taken place the 25th June, 1594. This rapid fucceffion is a fufficient proof of the immediate popularity of the poem.

The text of this edition generally coincides with that of the Firft; but the occafional deviations are always improvements, which feems to fhow that this impreffion, like the Firft, had the benefit of the author's revifion—a fact interefting on feveral accounts. In this opinion I am confirmed by the authority of a moft competent judge, Mr. J. P. Collier, who, after declaring his mature conviction, that in no inftance did Shakefpeare authorize the publication of a play, but allowed moft mangled and deformed copies of feveral of his greateft works to be circulated for many years, without expofing the fraud—an indifference fhared by many, if not by moft, of his contemporaries—feels quite as ftrongly convinced with refpect to the poems, efpecially "Venus and Adonis," and "Lucrece," that Shakefpeare, being inftrumental in their publication, and more anxious about their correctnefs, did fee, at leaft, the firft editions through the prefs. Thefe alterations are perpetuated in the fucceeding impreffions. Among them I may notice the following :—Sign. A v. *rev.* (iine 123), where *be* is advantageoufly fubftituted for *are*, apparently on account of the collocation of three words of fimilar found, *where, there, are;* fign. A vi. *rev.* (line 186), *face, I* inftead of *face I;* fign. A viii. *rev.* (line 266), *girtbs* for *girtbes;* fign. B ii. (line 353), where *tender* feems, on a little confideration, an improvement on *tenderer;* fign. B ii. *rev.* (line 363) *alablafter* for *allablafter;* fign. B v. (line 484), *world* for *earth;* fign. C viii. *rev.* (line 1041), *ugly* for *ougly;* fign. D. iii. (line 1168), *fprung* for *fproong*, etc. The patron's name is here fpelled Wriothefly, inftead of Wriothefley, as in the firft edition. In fome other impreffions it appears as Wriotheflie—another proof of the unfettled orthography of that age.

# LIST OF EDITIONS.

## I.

VENVS AND ADONIS *Vilia miretur vulgus: mihi flauus Apollo Pocula Caſtalia plena miniſtret aqua.* LONDON Imprinted by Richard Field, and are to be ſold at the ſigne of the white Greyhound in Paules Church-yard. 1593. [4to. 27 leaves.]

This is the Firſt Edition, printed with remarkable accuracy, doubtleſs from the author's own manuſcript, by an excellent printer, Richard Field, a native of Stratford, and the ſon of the Henry Field, whoſe goods John Shakeſpeare was employed to value in 1592. To the circumſtance of the printer being the fellow-townſman and probably the friend and aſſociate of the poet, may be attributed the honour of his being entruſted with the pub-lication of the firſt work of the bard.

The printer's device is an anchor, with the motto, "Anchora Spei," which were adopted, with a ſlight alteration in the anchor, in conſequence of their having been uſed by his father-in-law, Thomas Vautrollier, a celebrated and learned printer, who reſided in Black Friars, and to whoſe buſineſs, at his death in 1589, Field ſucceeded and continued in till after 1600.

This poem was licenſed by the Archbiſhop of Canterbury (Whitgift), and entered in the Stationers' Regiſter the 18th April, 1593. It is dedicated, like the ſucceeding editions, to Henrie Wriotheſley, Earle of Southampton and Baron of Titchfield. This dedication, and that of the "Rape of Lucrece," which was pub-liſhed in the next year, to the ſame patron, are the only proſe com-poſitions of Shakeſpeare not in a dramatic form which have come down to us.

Only one copy of this Firſt Edition of the "Venus and Adonis" is known, forming part of the Malone collection, in the Bodleian Library, and for which that eminent critic gave £25. He had long been in ſearch of it, for in his preface, 1790, he regrets his not having been able to procure the "Firſt impreſſion." In 1866 a lithographic fac-ſimile edition was made by E. W. Aſhbee, at the expenſe of Mr. J. O. Halliwell: only 50 copies were printed, of which 19 were deſtroyed, and the impreſſions removed from the ſtones. This unique copy meaſures 7¾ by 5¼ inches.

ſtill remaining in it as before; but no knowledge was extant of their peculiar value. In this ſtate they remained till September, 1867, when Sir Charles Iſham requeſted me, as the repreſentative of the publiſhers of this work, to report upon his library generally, and I was thus ſo fortunate as to bring to light a collection, in its ſpecial features unequalled in extent, value, and importance, and which, but for this circumſtance, might have remained for many ſucceeding years unknown, " unhonour'd, and unſung."

The intereſt excited by the diſcovery of theſe books has led to the reprint of that volume, which is, on ſeveral accounts, the moſt precious of them all ; the firſt tract in it being a hitherto unknown edition of the earlieſt production of him whoſe name has been characteriſed as " the greateſt in our literature—as the greateſt in all literature," for whatever doubts may exiſt as to the dates of the compoſition and the publication of other works of Shakeſpeare, one thing ſeems certain, namely, that his " Venus and Adonis " was not only his firſt-publiſhed but his firſt-written work, partially, if not entirely, compoſed before he left Warwickſhire, and kept by him till an opportunity occurred of giving it to the world.

And, as my diſcovery of the edition of 1599 has altered the received chronology of the various early impreſſions, incidentally leading to the finding of another unknown edition; and, as my reſearches on the ſubject have enabled me to correct ſome errors in previous accounts of them, I purpoſe to preface the preſent reprint by a ſhort deſcription of each edition. Thoſe preſerved in the Britiſh Muſeum I have myſelf examined, and for careful accounts of the others I am indebted to Mr. H. S. Harper, of the Bodleian Library.

ciating with many of the literary charaƈters and printers of his day, and thus enabled him to acquire the many curious and rare books accumulated at Lamport. They were obtained moſt likely immediately on publication, and depoſited in this country-ſeat, where they were kept ſecure from depredation and ill-uſage, as well as from ſuch public calamities as the Fire of London and the Civil Wars, which wrecked irretrievably many fine colleƈtions, both in town and country.

The firſt colleƈtor and preſerver of theſe curious books, therefore, was Thomas Iſham, and his name and handwriting appear in ſome of the traƈts. Great additions, however, were ſubſequently made to the collection by his ſucceſſors, particularly by Sir Juſtinian Iſham, the fifth baronet, who built the library and altered the houſe to its preſent form in the time of King George I. It had, however, undergone various alterations and improvements in the time of Charles I., from a deſign by John Webb, the ſon-in-law of Inigo Jones. The library becoming too ſmall for the accumulations, a large quantity of the commoner works, with many other very old, and, to an inexperienced eye, comparatively worthleſs ones, moſtly in an unbound condition, were removed to a garret. This room was for many years kept carefully locked up, and was never allowed to be entered, Sir Juſtinian Iſham, D.C.L., who died in 1818, prohibiting to every one but the butler the uſe of the key, and that only after the Baronet had become too infirm to walk upſtairs himſelf. He was equally averſe to any uſe being made of the books in the large library below ſtairs. Since his time, however, the garret in queſtion has been thrown open and uſed for various purpoſes, the books

correctly defcribed as "unprecedented in literature," was an upper lumber-room, far away from the general library (alfo containing many valuable and rare old works), at Lamport Hall, near Northampton, a large and well-preferved manfion, remarkable within for its beautiful old Italian cabinets, Paliffy ware, paintings, and other precious works of art; and without, for its delightful gardens and fplendid rockery, which make it one of the glories of the county. The houfe, after being for more than three centuries the property of the Truffels, was through a daughter's marriage transferred to the family of Vere, Earl of Oxford, by whom it was fold to Sir William Cecil, and afterwards to two brothers, Robert and John Ifham, whofe progenitors had been extenfive landowners in Northamptonfhire even before the time of William the Conqueror. This John Ifham, Efq., a mercer, who became fole poffeffor about the year 1560, was the fourth fon of Eufeby Ifham, of Pytchley, and the founder of the Lamport branch of the family. He married Elizabeth, daughter of Nicholas Barker, citizen of London, and had by her feveral children, of whom Thomas, his eldeft fon, married Elizabeth, daughter of Chriftopher Nicholfon, and dying in December, 1605, left iffue one fon, John, who was knighted by King James I.

This Thomas Ifham appears, from the family records, to have been a man of confiderable literary acquirements, as well as an enlightened bibliomaniac. His grandfather, Nicholas Barker, was, there is reafon to fuppofe, one of the great family of Queen's printers of that name, who even before entering that profeffion, were perfons of rank and opulence. Thefe circumftances led, in all probability, to Thomas Ifham's affo-

# EDITOR'S PREFACE.

THE prefent volume contains accurate reprints of three very rare and important works, which I had the good fortune to difcover while examining the large collection of old books accumulated during a period of nearly one hundred and fifty years by fucceffive members of the ancient family of Ifham.

But this was far from being the only curious volume found on the fame aufpicious occafion, for, in addition to a large number of Poetical Works of the Elizabethan era, of the greateft rarity and value, there were brought to light upwards of a dozen contemporary works, chiefly poetical, hitherto utterly unknown to literature. All thefe volumes, with but flight exceptions, were in perfect and moft defirable condition, both infide and out, being either in the vellum binding of the period, or what was more remarkable, and almoft unexampled in the cafe of tracts of that age, in the pamphlet form, with the edges entirely uncut.

The fcene of this fingular difcovery, which has been

CHISWICK PRESS:—PRINTED BY WHITTINGHAM AND WILKINS, TOOKS COURT, CHANCERY LANE.

# VENUS AND ADONIS,

FROM THE HITHERTO UNKNOWN
EDITION OF 1599;

## THE PASSIONATE PILGRIME,

FROM THE FIRST EDITION OF 1599; OF
WHICH ONLY TWO COPIES
ARE KNOWN;

## EPIGRAMMES,

WRITTEN BY SIR JOHN DAVIES,

AND

## CERTAINE OF OVID'S ELEGIES,

TRANSLATED BY

CHRISTOPHER MARLOWE,

FROM A RARE EARLY EDITION.

EDITED BY CHARLES EDMONDS,

EDITOR OF THE POETRY OF THE
ANTI-JACOBIN.

## LONDON:

HENRY SOTHERAN AND CO., 136, STRAND.

1870.

Charles Edmonds

**Venus and Adonis, from the Hitherto Unknown ed. of 1599**
*The passionate pilgrime, from the first ed. of 1599; of which only two copies are known; Epigrammes*

ISBN/EAN: 9783337288969

Printed in Europe, USA, Canada, Australia, Japan

Cover: Foto ©Lupo / pixelio.de

More available books at **www.hansebooks.com**

www.ingramcontent.com/pod-product-compliance
Lightning Source LLC
Chambersburg PA
CBHW030022030726
47499CB00008B/3080